THE LAZYMAN'S GUIDE TO FINANCIAL FREEDOM

THE LAZYMAN'S GUIDE TO FINANCIAL FREEDOM

TEJINDER SINGH MOKHA

Worldwide Published by
Pendown Press

PENDOWN PRESS

An ISO 9001 & ISO 14001 Certified Co.,
Regd. Office: 2525/193, 1st Floor, Onkar Nagar-A, Tri Nagar, Delhi-110035
Ph.: 09350849407, 09312235086
E-mail: info@pendownpress.com
Branch Office: 1A/2A, 20, Hari Sadan, Ansari Road, Daryaganj, New Delhi-110002
Ph.: 011-45794768
Website: PendownPress.com

First Edition: 2021
Price: ₹259/-
ISBN: 978-93-91544-86-7

Layout and Cover Designed by Pendown Graphics Team
Printed and Bound in India by Thomson Press India Ltd.

CONTENTS

INTRODUCTION

Hi Friends,

As always, God has been really kind to me during this Corona year as I was forced to sit down and concentrate on knowledge upgradation and, therefore, successfully earned the Certified Financial Planner certification from FPSB–US. I also completed certification as Registered Retirement Advisor with PFRDA (Pension Fund Regulatory and Development Authority), India. Besides, I was able to complete my research on Asset Classes, which was pending for the last five years. I am glad because this research will change our investors' lives. As everyone was sitting at home and had access to the internet, I started conducting free Master classes for middle-income group people of India through which we want them to take control of their Financial Future. I want to reach one crore people of India through this free Masterclass. And now another long cherished dream is getting fulfilled of writing this book. I really thank God for all these blessings and progress in one single year. I feel privileged.

I help people in creating Passive Income. The beauty of Passive Income is that it is not dependent on you and you keep receiving income even when you are not working. Normally singers/ writers receive this income, but common people like us can also earn such income through investments.

My journey with Financial Instruments started when I was in school in 5th class. I saved ₹500/- in NSC from my pocket money. But, I made lots of Financial mistakes in my life. I invested in stocks–lost money, I made investment in Property–my broker made money, my Bank which gave loan–made money, everyone except me made money. I purchased an Insurance pension plan at age 27–my insurance company and broker (bank) made money. I bought insurance policies to save tax–my advisor made money. Then I purchased another property in 2011–that money completely died, even principal is not retrievable.

After this life, with the blessing of God, I started taking knowledge. Till this date, I was very busy in Job and dependent on other people for financial decisions. When I decided to know more about finances, I started with General Insurance Industry, Health Insurance, Life Insurance, Mutual Funds, Stocks and Real Estate. I went to the best to learn. I always believe in attending paid trainings; I believe nobody who is capable, will teach me for free. When I go for paid training, chances of getting value increase. I was already late in acquiring the knowledge and wanted to learn fast. But every Industry I went to, I could only meet the Sales people, who never gave me the real picture. Insurance people told me insurance is your need. Stock trading people told me this is the only way to get rich. Real Estate people said this is the best way to multiply money. But who will teach me?

No one. I have to learn all by myself. I was losing money instead of gaining it. I was getting frustrated. Then, I decided to understand one thing at a time. I spent one year knowing health insurance. I spent the next year on Life Insurance; I went into detail, attended training from the best in the Country, the so-called big icons of the Life Insurance Industry. I wanted to understand beyond their sales techniques. I tried to validate things by counter-checking through other people. I met 15-20 people in Life Insurance Industry who were experts and literally interrogated them. Then I studied Real Estate–national and international, and in the process, I attended seminars of the best in the world.

I went to listen to Robert kiyosaki at his live seminar. I attended paid training of Rohan Weera Singhe, an International Real Estate tycoon from the UK who also imparts training on Real Estate in India, UK, the US, Australia and Singapore. Then, I started meeting best of the best fund managers and advisors in Mutual Fund Industry. I met Ramdeo Aggarwal ji, I went to live seminars of Rakesh Jhunjunwala, Nilesh Shah, Prashant Jain and who's who of Mutual Fund Industry. Met them, listened to them, again and again. I went to Mumbai/Gujarat several times to meet these people and understand the intricacies. After doing all this, I gathered knowledge and I kept implementing each and every thing I learnt.

So, in the process of knowing implementing, testing and rejecting ideas, and then learning new concepts and repeating this process, I could find the secret formulae for Wealth Creation. This formula is very well known to super rich, it is very basic knowledge for them. They don't waste time. They have a culture where parents teach this to their kids, who almost become financially independent by the age of 30.

But irony is nobody teaches this to Salaried class. Our parents don't know these secrets and we are stuck. I belong to a typical salaried class family where it is considered a sin to take risk in life. We are taught to move on a proven track and not deviate. We are so much afraid of deviating that we create 10x value for employers, but still never get confidence to work for ourselves. And most of the people who leave job and start a business is when they are going through their bad patch in career. 95% people leave job at that time. But, that is the time when you are low on confidence. I suggest, leave job when you have adequate reserves in your bank account and when you have an adequate reserve of confidence; believe me that is the best way to start your Entrepreneurial journey.

In this book, I have revealed all the mistakes one should avoid while making Financial Decisions. I hope these lessons will be life changing for you. These are Golden Nuggets which I learnt by paying a very high price. It is said, "Ordinary people learn from their mistakes, extraordinary people learn from other people's mistakes." This book is very practical and all learning can be implemented with ease. If you implement learning from this book, this will increase your speed on the journey to Wealth Creation by atleast 10-15 years. The younger you are more impact this book will make on your Financial Future.

Just one advice before you start reading this book. To get the maximum value, you have to cook and eat Dal Makhani.

You must be wondering that Punjabis are promoting their dishes. No, my purpose is different; I am suggesting this so that you can concentrate on reading book without distractions when your belly is full.

Jokes apart, please understand that the best Dal Makhani is available at very special Kesar Da Dhaba at Amritsar. We also make Dal Makhani with the same ingredients at our home, but we never get the same taste. So, what is so special? The difference lies in the RECIPE. Same way, when we talk of Financial Products, there are only four Asset classes, viz. Debt (FD/ Bonds/Debentures), Gold, Equity and Real Estate. 95% of products world-over are based on these 4 Asset Classes. So, I will also talk on the basis of these four products, and here you may feel this is what I already know. Just remember that secret is in the RECIPE, not the ingredients.

–Tejinder Singh Mokha
Certified Financial Planner

CHAPTER 1

SAVE YOURSELF FROM SALESMEN

Imagine you are sitting in your office, door opens, a person enters with a Financial Product. Is this product good for you?

Can you guess?

What is the probability that it's a right product for you?

You are purchasing Financial Products like this...

Your friend sends a person, your Father sends a person, your Uncle sends a person, your brother/sister/relative sends a person. This person can be some agent or a banker. But, this person has one product he/she wants to sell to you. Is this a good product for you?

I will give you another example. Suppose you are two friends, of same age, getting same salary with same family size i.e. wife, two kids (same age), dependent parents...

Although, I know this is practically not possible, but still I want you to imagine that even if it is true, one friend wants to save money to buy a car in two years' time and another one is saving for his kids' education after 10 years. Do you feel they both can purchase same product for investment?

Yes or No?

If your answer is no... then you will be shocked to know that most of the people who approach you with Financial Products, have a pre-decided product for you that they offer as a solution to your requirement.

Problem is even more intense. Now, imagine that these two needs are not of two different friends, these are your needs. In real life, we have different needs at the same point of time. After two years you want to purchase a car, after 10 years you need money for your elder child's education, after 15 years for younger kid, 20 years later for their marriage, 25 years later for your retirement, maybe five years later for your house, 8 years later for starting business, 3 years later for foreign trip, so on and so forth...

So, how can I pick the right financial products? Is There a lot of confusion?

No, there is n't and the way out is very easy. Today, I am going to tell you the Secret Formulae of picking Financial Products. If I say that this is the only way then it will not be wrong. So, if you have only one path then it can't be wrong. Yes, picking financial products is not an art, but a Science. And today, you are going to learn this Science.

The Secret is nobody can guide you. No relative, no friend, no banker, no advisor. But then who will guide you?

The only thing that can guide you is:

Remember the example of Dal Makhani–ingredients and recipe. This will look very simple, but still it is rarely implemented.

The only thing that can guide you is:

"Your Goals"

How can my goals guide me? Good question!

Understand here: someone approaches me with ₹5 Lac for investment, what is the first question I will ask him?

For how much time do you want to Invest this money?

Now, this may look very silly for you because we save money for our security & emergencies. How do we know when will that need originate?

Great!!

Now understand, your first goal is to create an Emergency Fund and have Health Insurance (Read chapter 4 for more details). All savings over and above this amount will be invested according to your Goals. You need to divide your goals into Short-Term Goals and Long-Term Goals:

First of all, write down all your goals which are priority now.

S.No.	Goal Description	No. of Years from now	Short Term/ Long Term
1.	Purchasing Car	1 year	Short Term
2.	Foreign Travel	1.5 year	Short Term
3.	Starting business	4 years	Short Term
4.	Buying a house	10 years	Long Term
5.	Kids higher education	12 years	Long Term
6.	Financial Freedom/ Retirement	20 years	Long Term

Short-Term Goals: Below 5 years

Long-Term Goals: Above 5 years

Now, please understand why we are dividing our goals under 2 categories. Because, priority and approach for these two categories are different.

For Short-Term Goals–Below 5 years, your priority is:

Priority No.	Priority Name
1	Security
2	Liquidity
3	Last is ....Return

So options here are:

Option 1	FD
Option 2	Debt Mutual Funds

For Long-Term Goals–Above 5 years, your biggest priority is to beat inflation post tax. Means Real Return should be Positive. What is real return? Real return is return that we get post Income Tax and post Inflation. If Real Return is not positive, your money is actually de-growing. Find below the real return of all popular Asset classes used for Investment. Here, we assumed inflation as 5%:

S. No.	Asset Class	Expected Return	Post Tax	Post Inflation
1.	FD	5.00	3.50	-1.50
2.	Debt Mutual Funds	5.50	5.00	0.00
3.	LIC	4.00	4.00	-1.00
4.	PPF	7.00	7.00	2.00
7.	Gold	6.00	5.50	0.50
5.	Real Estate	12.00	10.00	5.00
6.	Equity/Equity MF	12.00	10.80	5.80

Real Estate and Equity are volatile but they can give real return. Whether you want to invest in them or not, it is your choice. But I suggest that you start taking the knowledge on these Asset Classes.

CHAPTER 2

SAVE TAX ON FD INTEREST IT WILL SAVE YOU ₹1 CRORE MINIMUM

Do you know Govt. is not asking you to pay tax on FD interest that you get?

Is it really possible?

Yes, there is a way out. Remember Dal Makhani example and continue reading. You can invest in similar asset class as FD and save tax too.

Which is this Asset Class?

Name of this amazing Asset Class is Debt Mutual Funds.

They invest in FD, Bonds, Debentures and Govt. Securities. Actually FD has two peculiar features:

1. Fixed Date of Maturity
2. Fixed Rate of Interest

FD means when you give a loan to a bank. So, when you provide loans to Public Sector Undertakings (NHAI/REC...)/ Corporates (Tata Steel/Reliance Jio/.....) & Government (Central and State), these two features are part of every instrument. That is why we say similar Asset Class as FD.

But the question is- how you can save Tax?

In the case of Debt Mutual Funds, if you stay for longer than three years, you get indexation benefit. This means tax is not payable on full return. Suppose you get 7% return on Debt Mutual Fund, and inflation is 5% during the last three years, you will have to pay tax on only 2%. And that too at not 30%, but 20%.

		Investment Amount	**7% Return**	**Tax Paid 30%**	**Post Tax Return**
1.	FD	₹10,00,000	₹70,000	₹21,000	₹49,000
2.	Debt Mutual Fund	₹10,00,000	₹70,000	₹4,000	₹66,000
				Tax Saving	₹17,000

In the above chart, you can see that in FD you pay ₹21,000 tax on FD of ₹10 Lac and in Debt Mutual fund you pay ₹4k tax. (Inflation taken as 5% and tax as 30%)

One thing that you need to know here is the Portfolio of Debt Mutual Fund. Debt Mutual Fund invests with/gives loan to Government or Bank or PSU or Corporate, and the risk is very different across categories. Please understand Risk before investment.

Now you may not feel interested in ₹17,000/. Why should you bother to learn new thing for just ₹17,000/? What if I tell you this taxation will be minimum ₹1 crore in your lifetime!!

Yes, this knowledge is worth ₹1crore. Are you interested now?

We have taken an example of family which earns ₹1 Lac monthly and saves approx. 20k monthly. Their annual saving is ₹2.40 Lac. Suppose they invest in FD then after 1 year they get ₹2,53,440/- and in Debt MF they get ₹2,59,200/-, difference is ₹5,760/-. Nobody is interested for this 6-7k. But, practically speaking we have working age of 30 years, and we will keep investing in FD for these 30 years. Then after 30 years your maturity in FD is ₹1,86,80,520/- and in Debt MF it is 2,93,63,008, yes difference is ₹1,06,82,488/-.

Now, imagine if you are ignoring this information then it is costing you ₹1 crore.

Further, if you are earning ₹1 lac today your income and saving will increase in times to come, and it will be much higher after five years from now, and multifold after 10 years from now. So, difference will be much higher than ₹1 crore for you.

Year	Investment	FD	Debt MF	Difference
Return		8.00%	8.50%	
Post Tax Return		5.60%	8.00%	
1	₹2,40,000	₹ 2,53,440	₹ 2,59,200	₹ 5,760
5	₹2,40,000	₹14,17,299	₹ 15,20,623	₹ 1,03,324
10	₹2,40,000	₹ 32,78,448	₹ 37,54,917	₹ 4,76,469
15	₹2,40,000	₹ 57,22,446	₹ 70,37,828	₹13,15,382
20	₹2,40,000	₹ 89,31,820	₹1,18,61,501	₹29,29,681
25	₹2,40,000	₹1,31,46,261	₹1,89,49,060	₹58,02,799
30	₹2,40,000	₹1,86,80,520	₹2,93,63,008	₹1,06,82,488
35	₹2,40,000	₹2,59,47,921	₹4,46,64,516	₹1,87,16,594
	₹84,000,00			

Now, somebody will say I am already 50 years of age. This information is not of much benefit to me. No, you are doing a mistake!

First of all you can use this knowledge for next 10 years till retirement and further post 55 or 60 when you retire, Debt MF is of even more significance to you as your risk appetite reduces with age. If you survive till 80 as per average age estimate, then you will also use this information for at least 30 years and will reap equal benefits.

Imagine, two colleagues - Rahul and Raj-earning the same salary and saving equal amount, monthly. Rahul invests in FD, and Raj invests in Debt Mutual Funds for Retirement. Post-retirement (after 30 years), Rahul will get ₹1.86 crores and Raj will get ₹2.93 crores.

Will there be any difference in their standard of living?

CHAPTER 3

NOT INVESTING IN EQUITY IS INJURIOUS TO YOUR FINANCIAL HEALTH

Inflation word is normally heard in India during elections. Many a people feel inflation happens only in case of Onions. This is what our TV channels tell us. All other kinds of inflation are given least importance.

But in case of our Long Term Goals beating inflation is very important. Why?

In the above chapter, we have seen that FD is giving return of 5%. If we reduce tax it becomes 3.50% and if we reduce 5% inflation, this return becomes minus 1.50%. Now, imagine my Son receives ₹10 lac from his Grand parents, for his higher education and he invests in FD. Can you imagine what will be the value of ₹10 lac after 15 years, when he will actually need it?

In rupee terms, its value is ₹14.10 Lac, but considering today's purchasing power, this ₹14.10 lac will be equivalent to ₹8.59 Lac after 10 years.

So, now you understand why you should beat inflation for long term goals.

Let us understand further, in same example of FD vs Debt Mutual Fund, let's take.

Year	Investment	FD	Debt MF	Equity MF
Return		8.00%	8.50%	15%
Post Tax Return		5.60%	8.00%	13.50%
1	2,40,000	₹2,53,440	₹2,59,200	₹2,72,400
5	2,40,000	₹14,17,299	₹15,20,623	₹17,82,826
10	2,40,000	₹32,78,448	₹37,54,917	₹51,40,886
15	2,40,000	₹57,22,446	₹70,37,828	₹1,14,65,990
20	2,40,000	₹89,31,820	₹1,18,61,501	₹2,33,79,699
25	2,40,000	₹1,31,46,261	₹1,89,49,060	₹4,58,19,876
30	2,40,000	₹1,86,80,520	₹2,93,63,008	₹ 8,88,87,282
35	2,40,000	₹2,59,47,921	₹4,46,64,516	₹16,77,00,450
	84,00,000			

Imagine three colleagues Rahul, Raj and Shahrukh earning same salary and saving equal amount monthly. Rahul invests in FD, Raj in Debt Mutual Funds and Shahrukh invests in Equity Mutual Funds for Retirement. Post-retirement, after 30 years, Rahul will get ₹1.86 crores, Raj will receive ₹2.93 crores and Shahrukh gets ₹8.81 crores.

Now think of difference in Standard of Living and Lifestyle of these three people.

I am not asking you to put all your money in Equity Mutual Funds. But I am asking you a question that is it worth taking information on this asset class called Equity Mutual Funds?

The biggest question which comes to our mind here- "Is this 15% return possible?"

Yes, this 15% return is average return of Sensex for last 41 years:

Year	Sensex	Investment
1979	100	₹1,00,000/-
2020	38628 (31 Aug. 2020)	₹3,86,28,000/-

This is exactly 15.64% CAGR.

This return comes with a lot of risk and Mutual Fund helps to reduce risk, but cannot eliminate it 100%. Mutual Funds invest your money in the same equity market, but they hire experts, so they manage it far better.

15 Years Equity MF Performance			
15 Years Equity MF Performance	₹1 LAC BECAME	RETURN (%)	TIMES(X)
Average of Largecap Funds	₹6,89,154	13.73	6.9
Average of Blend/ Multicap Funds	₹7,02,837	13.88	7.0
Average of Mid/ Smallcap Funds	₹8,49,305	15.33	8.5
Average of All Diversified Equity Funds	₹7,25,319	14.12	7.3
Average of ELSS	₹6,91,665	13.76	6.9
Average of Aggressive Hybrid Funds	5,78,838	12.42	5.8

Data as on 31 Dec, 2019.

MF has multiplied wealth by seven times in the last 15 years!!

In this chart, you can see that Diversified Mutual Funds on an average, have given 14.12% CAGR return.

To improve your chances of getting 15% return, you need to follow the following principles:

1. Invest only through Mutual Funds. No direct equity investment.
2. Invest regularly through SIP.
3. Invest if your goal is minimum 8-10 years away from now.
4. Be Prepared, Market can fall anytime even without reason and Downfall may stay from 1-3 years.
5. Start looking for good exit point 2-3 years before your goal.

CHAPTER 4

BEFORE BUILDING YOUR PALACE OF DREAMS, LAY STRONG FOUNDATION

We all love to talk about our goals like building our house, sending kids for higher Education abroad, their marriage, our Financial Freedom. This is like constructing a Palace of Dreams...

What if something happens to the main bread-earner of the family?

If someone in family suffers a big Medical Emergency, all your life's savings can be spent on that.

In case of Accident, bread-earners can suffer some sort of disability which can cease the source of the only income.

What if your dream house that you have built with loan money, comes down due to Earthquake or a Tsunami?

All these risks are real and can affect your life, but the good part is there is a solution for all of them.

And the solution is Insurance. It means by paying some premium, your risk is transferred to the Insurance Company. And these are not very costly insurances.

A few tips wrt to insurance policies are as follows:

Life Insurance:

- Always declare true picture of your health and your smoking/drinking habit. Maximum claims are rejected because of non-declaration.
- Take it from good company with good Claim Settlement Ratio.
- Some people get confused how much insurance they should take. It should ideally be total of your liabilities like Kids' Education expense + Kids Marriage Expense+ Loan Outstanding+ Retirement Corpus required for your spouse. Take present cost. You need to deduct existing Assets/savings/investments and existing Life Insurance from this amount.

Health Insurance:

- Always declare your health issues, otherwise even after 10 years, the claim can be rejected on account of misleading the company at time of taking the policy.
- Take adequate health insurance. Today, everyone should have at least ₹10 lac insurance and ideal health insurance amount must be ₹20-50 Lac.

- Take insurance from company which will renew it for you for lifetime. Some companies don't renew policies post age 70 or 75.
- Understand all terms and conditions in detail.

Disability Insurance

- Must take Loss-of-Pay in case of an Accident. In this, till the time you are bed- ridden, insurance company pays you a part of your salary.

Home Insurance:

- This is very economical insurance.
- For ₹10,000 you can get your house insured.
- Rest premium depends on the benefits you add in the policy.

I have seen that some people love insurance policies and are over insured. I must tell them that insurance is not for benefit, purchasing extra insurance than required, is like purchasing a lottery on your life.

On the other hand, some people hate insurance and never get insured. I believe insurance should be adequate.

Some people say Insurance is an expenditure. Please understand that insurance is an expenditure till you don't need it. Secondly, people say I am healthy now, will take insurance when my health is not good. Please understand insurance is available only for healthy people; no company gives insurance when you are not well.

As per international standards, Insurance is quite economical in India,and you can easily transfer your life's risks to an Insurance Company.

CHAPTER 5

BIGGEST MISTAKE THAT PEOPLE MAKE WHILE PURCHASING THEIR DREAM HOUSE

I believe every Indian who is earning and is in the age group of 35-40, wants to purchase their own house. This is a very emotional decision for almost all Indians.

But, what is the problem in purchasing your own house?

Please understand I don't have any problem with you purchasing a house. The problem lies in the fact that people cannot judge the place they can afford. What does this mean?

At the age of 35-40, couple has already worked for 10-15 years and, therefore, must be having some savings. Let's assume, these savings are ₹50 Lac. By this time person is earning well so bank is ready to offer Loan of ₹50 Lac with EMI of ₹50k. per month. So, people feel they can afford house of ₹1 crore. No........... they will not stop here. Wife will sell her jewellery of ₹15 Lac. to buy house, parents and in-laws also offer loan, so person picks ₹25 Lac loan from relatives. Now, the person feels he has this ₹1.40 crores and he can afford house of the same amount.

But, this is a blunder.

Why?

Because your Emergency Fund will reach Zero. You had that ₹50 Lac savings for all your goals like Kids' Education, their Marriage, your retirement, etc. That ₹50k monthly saving is also cumulative for all the above-mentioned goals.

By my rough estimate, 50% of people in India commit this mistake. Now, if you need some money, will you sell one room of your house? The second alternative is to sell that house, use some amount for kids' education and move to a smaller place. Is it practically feasible?

In above mentioned case, I would suggest couples to contribute ₹20 Lac lump sum to buy a house and take loan of ₹20 Lac with EMI of ₹20k. So, in total you can afford house of 40lac and not ₹140 lac.

There are hundreds of cases in India where people have a house but no source of income post retirement. Now, kids live with you in your home, but you are dependent on them for your daily needs.

Is this good planning?

CHAPTER 6

WEALTH CREATION IS FIGHT BETWEEN GREED AND FEAR

I will not be wrong if I say that you are the biggest problem in your Wealth Creation.

No... No... No... How is this possible? How can you say that??

Please read on... you will get the answer. We may not know that the biggest enemies of our Wealth Creation are in your own heads. Do you want to know their names?

Greed and Fear.

Yes, this is true. You may agree or not. But sometimes you operate out of greed and make a loss and sometimes you operate out of Fear, and then also make a loss.

No, I am not like that. You need to prove.

Ok, let me explain with example.

When your brother tells you that he has made money from real estate, how do you feel? You go to the office and your colleague tells you he invested in real estate and made profits, how do you feel? You go to your doctor and he also says he made profit from real estate. You open the news channel and they are telling that property prices in all cities rose 100% in the last two years, and in the next two years, they will further double. This is the limit, you feel you are the only person left who has not made money from the real estate. The next day, you start searching for the property, take a loan and invest within next 15 days.

This is good…………… What is wrong in doing this?

Problem is that you have not done any research and you just purchased on the basis of what you heard from your circle and news channels. Now, as the market had already reached its peak, it starts falling, your property price of ₹1 crore comes down to ₹95 Lac in the next three months; you wait and you understand that prices go up and down. Then in next one year, prices fall further down to ₹80 Lac. You get restless, but you console yourself that "I should wait for some more time." Then in next six months prices go further down to ₹75 Lac, you are paying heavy EMI on that property and you had planned that prices will go up and you will sell the property and get out of it. Now you switch to same news channels and they are saying that due to Corona or Demonetisation, property prices will go further 25% down. This is the final wake up call for you and you immediately call your broker and sell that property for ₹75 Lac and get out of that.

Who forced you to take a wrong decision in this scenario? It is your atmosphere, your friends, colleagues, newspapers, news channels, everyone contributed. But main culprit which forced you to purchase at high was your Greed and what forced you to sell at low was your FEAR.

If you introspect, this is the reality. I see people going through it on a daily basis. Rather, I have seen the more intelligent a person is, the more he is influenced by Greed and Fear. And the problem is, once greed and fear take control, you become asymptomatic 'corona' patient, means you are not aware you are in their control. Even if someone tells you at that time, you will not agree with that person.

And this Greed and Fear may affect you not only in Real Estate, but in case of Equity as well as Gold.

Just for your respite, I am telling you that one of the most intelligent persons on Earth also suffered from same problem which affects you and me. You want to know his name?

His name is Albert Einstein. He invested much of his 1921 Nobel Prize money in **stock** markets. However, he **lost** a bulk of it in the **stock** market crash in 1929.

What is the solution?

"Awareness" is the only solution. You need to check at time of every big financial decision, if you are being motivated by Greed/Fear. If yes, wait and take more information, look into the facts.

Yes, I am saying Facts not Opinions.

CHAPTER 7

UNDERSTAND FINANCIAL FREEDOM

Many people feel Financial Freedom is a very fancy word and is not practical. So for your understanding, I am giving a very simple definition of Financial Freedom. Until and unless it is clear, you will not work towards it, however beautiful it may seem.

> *"Financial Freedom is the age after which you don't want to work for money."*

I am 43 today and I want that I should be financially free by 50. Does this mean that I will not work post 50?

Absolutely NO.

I want to work till I survive maybe 70 or 80 or till my last breathe, but what I want is that I should do only that work which I enjoy. Today I enjoy doing Financial Planning, maybe at age of 65 my health may or may not allow me to work. At that time I can reduce my working hours. At that time I may feel like playing Golf full time. I will do something which will give me pleasure; I will not work for money then.

Hope this clarifies Financial Freedom to you too.

I must tell you that Financial Freedom is a very beautiful concept; the earlier you can achieve it, the better it is. As you have seen in 3 *Idiots* movie, R. Madhavan wants to opt for wildlife photography. There are many Madhavans in this world who are actually Engineers, whose parents had not seen 3 *Idiots* movie. These Madhavans can achieve Financial Freedom and then pursue their passion during this lifetime. So no need to kill your dreams now; keep it alive, work hard, save more, be financially free and then live a life of your dreams.

Now that you want to be Financially Free very soon, and have no idea on how to go ahead, I will explain in detail. For simplification, I have divided Financial Freedom into three parts:

Stage–I

Expense Replacement or Job Freedom: For those who are looking to leave job and start business, the first step is to create a corpus which is sufficient enough to give you monthly expenses. Understand beforehand that it will take at least two years to come to the same income level which you were getting in the Job. During these two years, in order to have peace of mind, create a corpus which keeps giving you amount equivalent to your monthly expenses + EMI.

Stage–II

Income Replacement: Second Level to be achieved after expense replacement is Income Replacement. You were able to generate an amount equal to expenses earlier, now increase your investment and when your investments start giving you return equivalent to your income, you can say you have achieved Income Replacement.

Stage–III

Complete Financial Freedom: This is the biggest goal. Here, your investments should give you an income and also increase as per inflation. So, your income from investments should increase at the rate of inflation. If you are getting ₹1 Lac today and you get the same money even after ten years, the purchasing power of ₹1 Lac may have reduced to ₹70k.

Why Financial Freedom/Retirement is a very big goal?

1. **Inflation** increases your Pension requirement every year. My father retired in 1999 and he was getting a pension of ₹17k. In Government pension increases with the increase in Inflation. My father's pension today is ₹65k. If he still keeps getting ₹17k, he can't maintain same standard of Living. Same way, you also need pension with Inflation. Inflation makes it very huge.
2. **Average Age:** In India, average age as of now is 68 years, but in the areas where we have better hygiene and medical facilities, average age is 75 already. This is further increasing very fast, in developed countries like the US, it's already 82 years and in Japan it's 87 years. It is expected to increase further in India as well. Imagine, people losing jobs in Corona and in three months they could not manage finances, we are talking of stopping work and eating for next 30 years. It is not a small goal! Can you see it?

Tips to youngsters for Financial Freedom:

1. Start parking amount for Financial Freedom right from day 1 when you start earning. If you are already past that time, teach this to your kids.
2. 50% of your savings should go for Financial Freedom and the rest 50% should be used for all other goals like building a Dream House, Kids' Education, Kids' Marriage, Purchasing Cars, going on Foreign Trips, etc.

CHAPTER 8

HOW TO REDUCE RISK AND INCREASE RETURNS ON YOUR PORTFOLIO

Every person who invests has a secret desire to increase returns to the maximum and reduce risk to a minimum. This is what we understood in the chapter of Greed and Fear. But there are some techniques, which can be used to achieve this beautiful wish.

We all have heard the famous saying that don't put all your eggs in one basket, but how can we implement it in our investments? The solution is Asset Allocation.

Asset Allocation			
Year	Equity	Gold	FD
2001	-21.60%	11.60%	9.25%
2004	13.70%	1.78%	5.38%
2008	-44.04%	23.64%	8.63%
2011	-5.57%	41.54%	7.88%
2014	45.03%	-0.42%	8.53%

This chart shows calendar year returns. You can see the years when equity has given negative returns, Gold/FD has given positive returns. Years when Gold has not given any returns, Equity and FD has given good ones.

Therefore, when you use Asset Allocation, it reduces your risk and increases chances of getting positive returns.

But the real secret is if you use it with a great friend of Asset Allocation, it increases the benefits multi-fold if used in tandem. This great friend is Rebalancing.

Rebalancing Asset Allocation					
		Equity % age	Equity	Debt	Total
Jan 2007		70%	₹7,00,000	₹3,00,000	₹10,00,000
Jan 2008	E: 62.51% D: 8.07%	78%	₹11,37,570	₹3,24,210	₹14,61,780
Jan 2008-Reb		70%	₹10,23,246	₹4,38,534	₹14,61,780
Jan 2009-Reb	E: -57.13% D: 8.06%	48%	₹4,38,666	₹4,73,880	₹9,12,546
Jan 2010	E: 88.57% D: 6.47%	70%	₹6,38,782	₹2,73,764	₹9,12,546
			₹12,04,551	₹2,91,476	₹14,96,027

In the above-mentioned example, you have rebalanced your portfolio back to 70% equity and 30% debt every year. Maturity amount here is ₹14.96 Lac, whereas without rebalancing this amount will be only ₹12.92 Lac.

CHAPTER 9

SECRET TO WEALTH CREATION IS MAKING A START

Rest all is *gyan* (knowledge) till you implement it. The only most important thing for Wealth Creation is making a START.

If you are thinking that you have understood the concepts and will start very soon or you will start as soon as possible to save, I am sorry to say, you are very wrong. You have to make a start and then the path will get clearer.

No, No, I am serious, but I don't have savings, I can't make a start right now.

At this point, my question to you is that do you have the intent? If yes, I am going to help you in Saving also. You have to do an exercise using the following table:

MONTHLY CASH FLOW STATEMENT					
INCOME			**EXPENSES**		
Self			Petrol Diesel		
Spouse			Rent/Maintenance		
Rent			Electricity/Water		
Other			Milk		
Bonus		Annual/12	Ration/Fruits/Veg		
EPF			Mobile/internet		
			School Fees/tutionetc		
			Maid/Driver		
			Eating Out/ Entertainment		
			Shopping		Annual/12
			Gifts		
			Travel		Annual/12
			Insurance		Annual/12
			Parents		
			Medical Exp		
			Car EMI		
			House EMI		
Income Total			**Expenses Total**		
			INVESTMENT		
			EMI 2nd house		
			LIC		
			SIP		
			RD		
			PPF		
			EPF		
			Investment Total		
			Additional Saving		

I suggest you make a cash flow of your income and expenses as per above- mentioned table; whatever comes as Additional Savings is anyway that you can save. (Income Total – Expenses Total – Investment Total = Additional Savings).

If you want to save more, you can reduce your expenses under the following heads:

1. Petrol/Diesel
2. Eating out/Entertainment
3. Shopping
4. Travel

Another mistake that people make is they save whatever is left at the end of the month. They use following formulae:

Income–Expenses = Savings

By above formulae savings always comes as Zero. If you really want to save, park some amount in second bank account at start of the month. Change formulae to following:

Income – Savings = Expenditure

Spend what is left post saving.

This way you will not only be able to make a start at Investments but with time and little effort, you will achieve your goals as well.

Just to show you benefit of starting early, I am putting here an example. If three friends are saving for retirement, Rahul starts at 35, Raj a year prior to him Shahrukh five years prior to Rahul:

Start Age	Saving	Retirement Corpus at 60	Difference
Rahul - 35	₹20,000	₹5,51,31,216	
Raj - 34	₹20,000	₹6,36,59,982	₹85,28,766
Shahrukh - 30	₹20,000	₹11,26,35,408	₹5,75,04,193

Rahul gets Corpus of ₹5.51 cr, Raj gets ₹85 Lac extra just by starting a year prior to him and Shahrukh gets ₹5.57 crores extra just by starting five years prior to Rahul (Return calculated at 15% pa).

Now you decide whether you want to be Rahul, Raj or Shahrukh among your friends?

CHAPTER 10

HOW TO CHOOSE A GOOD FINANCIAL ADVISOR

Once you reach to the point where you start earning and can save a little—get a financial advisor to educate you and help make decisions; the earlier the better.

But before doing that understand the role of a Financial Advisor in your life:

1. **Trustworthy:** If choice is between intelligent or trustworthy, choose trustworthy.
2. **Qualification:** Normally Financial advisors are CFPs, IA (Investment Advisor)– I & II or Certified Retirement Advisor. You can check their qualification, as this ensures minimum level of skill.

3. **Experience:** In this industry, a person learns more by experience rather than through books. How many market falls your advisor has seen or survived is very important. Every market cycle gives new learnings. As it is said, many Captains of opposition cricket teams retire immediately after Australia tour, same way many Financial Advisors leave industry at the time of equity market declines. Their long term continuity is of paramount importance. And if he/she has survived for 15-20 years that means they have the grit and determination to learn, grow and survive. This Industry goes through radical change every 5 years.
4. **Mutual Fund scheme selection criteria.** You need to know on what basis your Financial Advisor selects the mutual fund schemes. If they are just looking at past returns, they are not justifying their job. They need to understand the risk and explain you the same as well.
5. **Asset Allocation:** Understand their system of Asset Allocation. As this is biggest tool to reduce risk and volatility in a portfolio.
6. **Rebalancing:** Understand their system of rebalancing as this not only reduces risk but increases chances of return in long term.
7. **Online Platform:** Today, most of the Industries are working online, your distributor should also be updated. Mainly, two platforms are being used in India, one is BSE other is NSE, and both are equally good.
8. **Team:** You can understand their team structure as this ensures continuity of services in the future.

9. **Calm Mind:** This is most important criteria for me when selecting a Financial Advisor as I need a guide who is not impacted by greed and fear himself. He/ She should be able to maintain their cool under all circumstances.

Based on the above selection criteria you should select Financial Advisor. He/She is the person who hand-holds you at time of market falls, when you are being impacted by Greed & Fear, he/she reminds you of your goals so that you don't get affected by short-term events like Corona or demonetisation. Financial Advisor is like a Sherpa, who helps you reach Mount Everest like personal goals/dreams.

CHAPTER 11

RECAP

I am really glad you have reached the last page of this Book. Let us have an insight of major learning that we had till now:

- You learnt that defining your goals is the first step before looking for products which best suit your requirement. Chances of mis-selling get very low.
- You have demarcated your goals under short-term and long-term categories plus you learnt what are the Investment Options for Short-Term goals-below 5 year, and Investment Options for Long-Term goals-above 5 year.
- You learnt benefits of Investment in Debt Mutual Funds over FD.
- You learnt benefits of Equity Mutual Funds and how much difference they can make in your life. Plus, how important it is to take knowledge on Equity Mutual Funds.

- You learnt that laying strong foundation is most important before building your Palace of dreams like (Kids Education, Financial Freedom etc…).
- You learnt what mistake people make in building their dream house and how to avoid it.
- You learnt how to save yourself from Greed and Fear at the time of making Financial Decisions.
- You learnt what is Financial Freedom and its stages. You need to make a start from expense replacement.
- You learnt while managing money don't put all your eggs in one basket and use Asset Allocation and Rebalancing.
- Last thing you learnt is how making a START in itself is very important and that too early start like Shahrukh, and not like Rahul or Raj (Page 34).

Here, I would like to inform you that I have implemented all the learnings mentioned in this book in my own life and I am really glad with the outcome. Not only this, I have improved the Financial well-being of more than 250 families whose portfolios we manage currently.

Among them, one is Mr. Tarun, who is a senior professional in IT Sector. At age 45 this couple was not sure about achieving all their aspirational dreams of Kids' Higher Education, purchasing House and the biggest of all Financial Freedom. When finance becomes overwhelming, you have one solution–ignore it. They also followed this path for many years, but finally decided to take their Finances under their control, after attending my Masterclasses. After one month of attending sessions and one-two-one discussions/hand-holding sessions, today, they are very clear about their Financial Goals. They have prioritised their goals and reduced a few to make them practical and achievable. Not only this, they are also clear about how they are going to achieve them. Earlier they used to ignore Finances and now they get Peace of Mind by looking at them.

Another example is a Doctor who is single mother to a special child. Being a single mother requires you to manage finances properly and when the kid is a special child, you need to take extra care. She accepted the challenge to learn Finance and is, today, crystal clear about not only her Financial Security, but about her Son's Financial Security as well.

The Ultimate Goal of Financial Planning is to achieve Peace of Mind.

Now, you have two choices:

1. Read this book again and again and implement the learnings, or
2. You can come to my Free Masterclass wherein we administer advanced knowledge related to Financial Management. This Masterclass will surely amplify your knowledge.

To attend my next masterclass, you can check our website:

www.tejindersinghmokha.com

Here, I am giving you my personal email id:

Tejinder@bachatguru.co.in

I am always available for my Readers. You can send me your feedback and if you have any specific question, I will try to answer it to the best of my ability.